E is for Extreme

An Extreme Sports Alphabet

Written by Brad Herzog and Illustrated by Melanie Rose

Sleeping Bear Press™

310 North Main Street, Suite 300
Chelsea, MI 48118
www.sleepingbearpress.com

© 2007 Thomson Gale, a part of the Thomson Corporation.

Thomson, Star Logo and Sleeping Bear Press are trademarks
and Gale is a registered trademark used herein under license.

Printed and bound in Canada.

First Edition

10 9 8 7 6 5 4 3 2 1

Library of Congress Cataloging-in-Publication Data

Herzog, Brad.
E is for Extreme : an extreme sports alphabet / written by Brad Herzog;
illustrated by Melanie Rose.
p. cm.
Summary: "Extreme sports and its many and varied activities are introduced
from A to Z using poetry, prose, and illustration in this children's picture book.
Topics include adventure racing, bungee jumping, freestyle skiing, the Iditarod,
and kiteboarding"—Provided by publisher.
ISBN-13: 978-1-58536-310-0
ISBN-10: 1-58536-310-3
1. Extreme sports—Juvenile literature. I. Rose, Melanie, ill. II. Title.

GV749.7.H47 2007
796.04'6—dc22   2006026986

For anyone who has ever scampered up the dunes, canoed to the lighthouse, paddled a playak, run the Luck of the Draw race, hiked through Pictured Rocks, braved a Big Trip, competed in pushball or speedball or Rindy ball, gone orienteering, windsurfed, skished or played archery golf at Camp Nebagamon in the North Woods of Wisconsin.

BRAD

For Gerry.

MELANIE

A
a

An adventure race is a nonstop, multi-sport event in which teams of one to five people travel through some of the most remote and challenging places in the world. Some races take only a few hours, while others last more than a week. The racers move along a series of checkpoints where they can replenish supplies, but they are expected to carry their own gear. Sports featured in adventure races have included running, rappelling, horseback riding, mountain biking, swimming, sea kayaking, whitewater canoeing, even scuba diving.

Many adventure races also require an element of orienteering, which is the ability to navigate using a map and compass in the wilderness. Several races—with exotic names like Eco-Challenge, Primal Quest, and The Raid—have become world-famous events held in places ranging from Morocco to Madagascar. But not all adventure races take place in remote wilderness. Some races through cities, like the Wild Scallion Race in Chicago, require skills ranging from scootering to stair climbing.

Catch air on a mountain bike.
Ascend a steep rock face.
Go all around the world.
A is an Adventure race.

B is for a Bucking Bronco
or a big, bad bull.
Eight seconds seems like forever
to make a ride in full.

Bronc riding is one of the most exciting events in rodeo (a Spanish word meaning "roundup"). Imagine sitting on an untamed bronco in a small enclosure known as a bucking chute. With one hand, you grip a special rigging or rope attached to the wild horse. You nod your head, the gate of the chute opens, and the bronco charges into the arena, attempting to throw you off in any way possible. You try to stay atop the animal for eight seconds without falling. Judges award points based on the performance of both the rider and the animal. A perfect score is 100 points. If the rider is bucked off or touches the animal or any of his equipment with his free hand, he receives no score.

Bull riding is even more dangerous, as brave cowboys climb atop angry, one-ton beasts with sharp horns. Often the bulls become as well-known as the cowboys. From 1984 through 1987 a famous bull named Red Rock bucked off everyone who tried to ride him—309 attempts altogether!

Bb

C is for Cycling coast-to-coast
without a moment to lose—
a chase across the continent,
hardly a pleasure cruise.

Every year a handful of courageous athletes compete in a remarkable ultracycling competition called the Race Across America (RAAM). It is a 3,052-mile, single-stage bike race from San Diego, California, to Atlantic City, New Jersey—a coast-to-coast journey through heat, humidity, hail, 50-mph headwinds, and combined climbs totaling some 110,000 feet. Each rider (or team of riders) is followed by a crew in a van that offers nutritional, medical, and mechanical aid. But the race still amounts to a test of mental and physical endurance.

Traditionally, the top competitors have ridden some 350 miles per day while averaging barely 90 minutes of sleep every 24 hours. Because the lack of sleep can be so dangerous (two riders have been struck by passing trucks), in 2006 race officials added a mandatory rest period each day for cyclists who wish to win prize money. But some riders still choose to compete in the Nonstop Record Category anyway. Finishing the race is their reward.

A day at the Drag races
that's our letter D.
At 300 miles per hour
they're the fastest cars you'll see.

Drag racing is loud, dangerous, and very fast. It usually involves two cars starting from a dead stop and racing over a short, straight course to see who crosses the finish line first. The winner moves on to the next heat until there is only one undefeated racer left. The most common distance is a quarter-mile course, although the drag strip extends beyond the finish line to allow cars to slow down. Drivers don't have to make any turns, but they must be able to react quickly, shift gears properly, and keep the car on course. There is no time to recover from mistakes.

The National Hot Rod Association (NHRA) oversees most drag racing events in North America and offers dozens of racing divisions, including a category for aspiring young racers—Junior Dragster. The fastest cars are Top Fuel dragsters, which look almost like rockets on wheels and can reach speeds of over 300 miles per hour and cover a quarter-mile distance in less than five seconds!

Dd

When mountaineer George Mallory was asked in 1923 why he wanted to climb Mount Everest, the world's highest peak at 29,035 feet above sea level, he answered, "Because it is there." Climbing Everest is extremely difficult and dangerous. Mallory was lost on the mountain one year after making his statement, and it wasn't until May 29, 1953 that Sir Edmund Hillary and Tenzing Norgay became the first men to conquer Everest. To date, about 1,000 people have managed the feat. The youngest was 15 years old!

Mountaineers, also known as alpinists, brave many perils (including falling rocks and ice, avalanches, deep crevasses, and severe weather). So they must select the best route up a mountain at the proper time of year. To avoid altitude sickness, climbers get accustomed to the lack of oxygen at loftier heights by sleeping at gradually higher base camps, sometimes even over the course of several weeks. Most mountaineers use bottled oxygen when climbing the highest mountains, like Everest.

E is Eager mountaineers
and an extreme test—
braving all the elements
to climb Mount Everest.

Perform a triple back flip
F with four twists as you go.
is Freestyle skiing—
acrobatics on snow.

Freestyle skiing is a combination of alpine skiing and acrobatics. Two Olympic sports fall under this category—aerial skiing and mogul skiing. Aerialists ski off jumps made of snow, soar more than 50 feet high, perform back flips and as many as four or five twists, and then land on an inclined hill. The skiers are judged on their takeoff, jump form, landing, and degree of difficulty. In mogul skiing, athletes ski down a steep slope covered with moguls (very large bumps). They are scored on their speed, technique, and two aerials that they perform on the way down the hill. Every freestyle skiing competition is a spectacular show.

F is also for free diving, which includes "apnea" competitions in which divers attempt to reach great depths on a single breath and without help from a breathing apparatus. In October 2005, Austrian Herbert Nitsch recorded a record depth of 564 feet in the Adriatic Sea.

F f

Look up in the sky!
Gee, what could that be?
A great leap with a bungee cord.
G is Gravity.

Bungee jumping is a dangerous activity in which a person leaps from a structure several hundred feet high, such as a bridge or a platform. One end of an elastic cord is attached to his or her body, and the other end is tied to the jumping-off point. As the person falls, the cord stretches as it adapts to the energy of the fall. When the cord snaps back, the jumper flies upward, moving up and down as the cord expends the energy. The first known bungee jump occurred in England in 1979, but the idea came from the South Pacific island nation of Vanuatu, where young men would show their courage by jumping from tall platforms with vines attached to their ankles.

G is also for the Gravity Games, a multi-sport event in which athletes compete in a variety of extreme sports, including street luge, skateboarding, wakeboarding, and freestyle motocross

Downhill skiers know that the best ski runs are often the first runs of the day. That's when the snow hasn't yet been packed down or rutted with tracks made by other skiers. So the early bird gets the best snow. But experienced skiers sometimes use another bird to locate deep, smooth "powder"—a helicopter! Helicopter skiing, or heli-skiing, is a way to reach remote backcountry slopes, where the powder is pristine.

H is for hefty. That's the cost of heli-skiing, which is expensive because the skiers stay in lodges and are shuttled back and forth by air for as many as five to twelve runs per day, each one on a fresh, untracked slope. **H** is also for hazardous. Heli-skiers (and heli-boarders) often make their way around huge trees and endure the constant threat of avalanches. However, reputable heli-skiing operations employ guides who are trained to judge snow conditions, so that the skiers can concentrate on the slopes.

No lifts, no lines, no crowds,
and perfect, untracked snow.
H is Helicopter skiing.
Fly up, climb out…then go!

Before airplanes and snowmobiles arrived, people relied on sled dogs to travel across the Alaskan wilderness during the winter. Every March since 1973 that important part of the state's history is honored by the Iditarod Trail Sled Dog Race, a 1,150-mile marathon from the city of Anchorage, in south central Alaska, to Nome, which is located on the western coast. Sled drivers, who are often called mushers, lead teams of 12 to 16 dogs over frozen rivers, through dense forests, and across windswept plains—all the while enduring temperatures far below zero. The dogs, usually Alaskan or Siberian Huskies, are specially bred to endure the elements, and each musher has his or her own strategy for training, feeding, and running them. Famous Iditarod champions include five-time winner Rick Swenson, four-time champ Susan Butcher, and Martin Buser, who won the 2002 race in record time—just under nine days. However, everyone who finishes the race is greeted by a cheering crowd in Nome—and the sound of the city's fire siren.

I i

I is the Iditarod,
a grueling sled dog race
across Alaskan ice
at an impressive pace.

Our J is a place called Jaws,
    where giant waves rise from the sea.
Watch the surfers from the beach.
    It's the safest place to be.

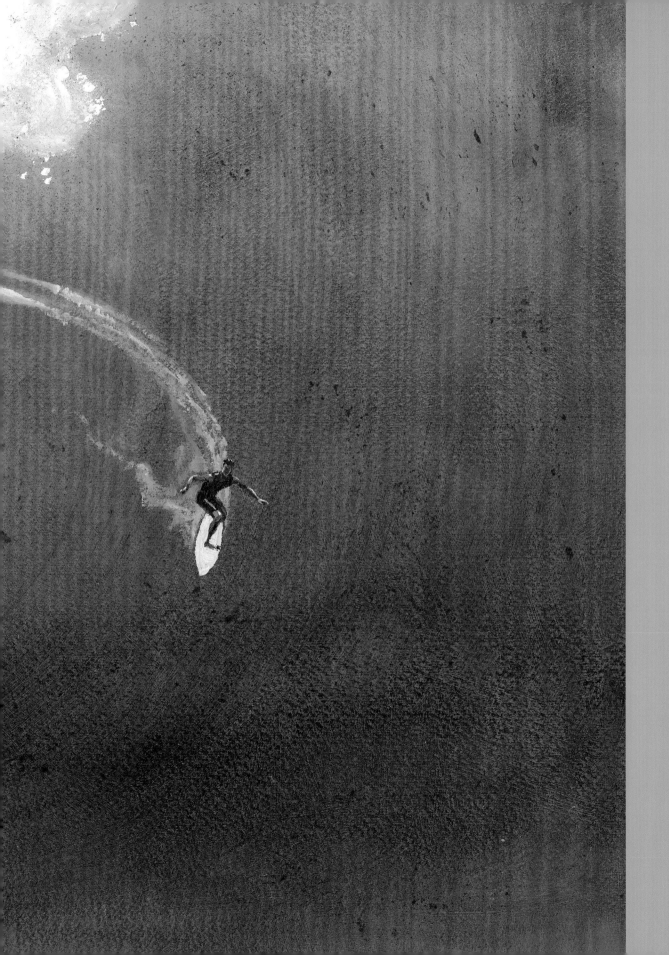

Big wave surfing is surfing with some extra danger on board. Using extra-long surfboards known as guns (which are more stable and faster-moving), riders paddle into waves at least 20 feet high. The boards are longer in order to allow the surfers to catch the bigger, speedier waves. When the surf is so imposing that it is impossible to paddle in, surfers may choose to use specialized boards fitted with foot loops. They are then towed into the big waves behind a jet ski.

The biggest waves can be found only in specific surfing spots, places with names like Billabong (in Australia) and Mavericks (in northern California). Jaws, also known as Pe'ahi, is located on the North Shore of the Hawaiian island of Oahu. When conditions are right, the waves there rise as much as 80 feet high! One surfer, Don Curry, has compared the big wave experience to "jumping off a four-story building, except the building is toppling toward you at incredible speed."

Jj

K is for Kiteboarding
on water, snow, or land.
Climb into a harness.
Let the winds give you a hand.

K k

Kiteboarding is simply using a kite to pull you on a board and letting the wind propel you to great speeds and heights. It can be done on water (kite surfing), on snow (snow kiting) or on land (sometimes known as land boarding). Kite surfing is basically a combination of wakeboarding and windsurfing. Snow kiting is essentially snowboarding with bigger air, thanks to Mother Nature. Land boarding requires a big skateboard with off-road wheels and open spaces with few obstructions, such as a large hard-packed sandy beach. Different sizes of kites allow people to enjoy the sport in various wind strengths. In general, bigger kites are used in lighter winds and smaller kites in stronger winds. Participants wear a harness, which is attached to the kite, and hold a control bar or handles to direct the kite. Because the kite is both a lifting force and a pulling force, experienced kiteboarders are often able to launch huge aerial maneuvers.

A luge is a small one- or two-person sled on which athletes speed down an icy course while on their back, feet first—and it's the name of the Olympic sport in which the sleds are raced. Street luge is a similar activity, only on pavement instead of ice. It may be best described as a gravity-powered sport in which competitors seek to move as fast as possible on what is basically an oversized skateboard.

Lugers wear helmets and face shields or goggles, as well as racing suits and gloves. On the board, their heads are slightly elevated so that they can see where they're going. Many boards have footrests, but lugers also use their feet to brake because mechanical brakes are prohibited. This is no easy feat when a street luge (also sometimes known as a land luge or road luge) can move as fast as 80 miles per hour!

Lie down on a skateboard
and look out below.
L is for street Lugers.
See how fast they go!

Ll

M m

Dramatic leaps! Spinning tires tossing dirt! Riders leaning into curves! Motocross is an exciting form of racing in which motorcycles or all-terrain vehicles speed around a large (usually a mile or more) naturally-formed track that often features several hills. The name of the sport (often abbreviated MX) is a combination of motorcycle and cross-country. A race is complete when the competitors (as many as several dozen at a time) finish a certain number of laps or when a fixed time period has passed (anything up to 40 minutes). A racer's total finishing place is usually determined by averaging the results from two or three race legs (called motos). The sport has evolved into several categories, including supercross (racing on a man-made track consisting of many jumps), supermoto (racing motocross bikes on track and pavement), and bicycle motocross (BMX) on shorter, slightly smoother tracks. In freestyle motocross (FMX) competitors perform acrobatic stunts while jumping motocross bikes.

M must be for Motocross
on a sandy, hilly track.
Make a mighty move
to break out from the pack.

When thrill-seekers use a parachute to jump from a fixed object it is called BASE jumping. The letters in BASE stand for the four types of objects from which one can jump—building, antenna, span (such as bridge,) and earth (any natural formation, such as a cliff). Because jumps are usually made from heights of less than 2,000 feet, it is actually more dangerous than skydiving. Jumpers must use a special fast-opening parachute, and there is no time to open a reserve parachute.

BASE jumping itself is not illegal, but jumpers must have permission to use both the jump platform and the landing area. Once a year, on the third Saturday in October, more than 400 BASE jumpers and thousands of spectators gather for Bridge Day in Fayetteville, West Virginia. The jumpers are given special permission to parachute from the New River Gorge Bridge, which is 876 feet above a river. There are also occasional BASE jumping competitions throughout the world in which jumpers are judged on accurate landings or freefall aerobatics.

N
n

The New River Gorge Bridge.
That's **N** in our alphabet.
Here, folks jump with parachutes,
but without a net.

O o

O, the mighty ocean.
Fight the choppy waves.
Open water swimming
is for the strong and brave.

Swimming long distances can be difficult. But imagine doing so when there are no walls to grab when you get tired, no way of seeing more than a few feet in front of you, cold and choppy water trying to splash in your mouth with every breath, and sea creatures—seen and unseen—lurking around you! That's open water swimming, a sport in which people swim across large bodies of water such as oceans, lakes, or rivers—usually without a wetsuit. There are organized competitions (the World Swimming Championship holds races of 5, 10, and 25 kilometers), but there are also many athletes who swim solo. Women, in particular, have had great success as open water swimmers. In 1926 Gertrude Ederle became world famous when she set a record for the fastest crossing of the 21-mile-wide English Channel—in under 15 hours. Current long-distance swimmer Alison Streeter has conquered the channel more than 40 times, including seven times in one year!

P is for a Powerboat
racing across a placid lake.
At more than 100 miles per hour
it produces quite a wake.

Almost ever since there have been motor-boats there have been motorboat races along lakes, rivers, and oceans. Today these vessels move so fast that they are known as powerboats. There are more than a dozen categories of powerboat racing, including a Formula 1 circuit (in which teams compete all around the world), offshore powerboat racing (involving large oceangoing boats), personal watercraft races (a bit like moto-cross on water), drag boat racing, and junior classes (for kids 9 to 15 years of age).

Boats in the Unlimited Hydroplane class, perhaps the best-known form of power-boat racing, have been described by the American Power Boat Association as "rocket ships on water." They reach remarkable speeds because only a tiny fraction of the boat touches the surface of the water during a race. Of course, great speeds come with great risk. To protect the drivers, cockpit capsules are designed to break away from the rest of the boat in a hard crash.

Since 1934 the Quebrada Cliff Divers in Acapulco, Mexico, have thrilled crowds with death-defying diving demonstrations off a rocky ledge. Five times each day these professional high divers swim across a 22-foot-wide canal, scale a 110-foot rock wall, pause to pray at a shrine atop the cliff, and then dive into the waters below. The cliff divers ("los clavadistas" in Spanish) must leap nearly 30 feet horizontally to avoid the rocks and must time their dives with an incoming wave to cushion the impact and protect them from landing in water that is too shallow. Because each diver hits the water at approximately 55 miles per hour, he must clench his fists to avoid broken fingers and must slice into the water at the proper angle to avoid shattered limbs. La Quebrada, where the World Cliff Diving Championships are held each year, means "the broken" in Spanish. That well describes the danger of the stunt.

Q is La Quebrada,
    a place in Mexico
where divers plunge from jagged cliffs
        into the sea below.

Reaching for the right hold,
Risking sudden falls,
R is for Rock climbing—
on boulders and sheer walls.

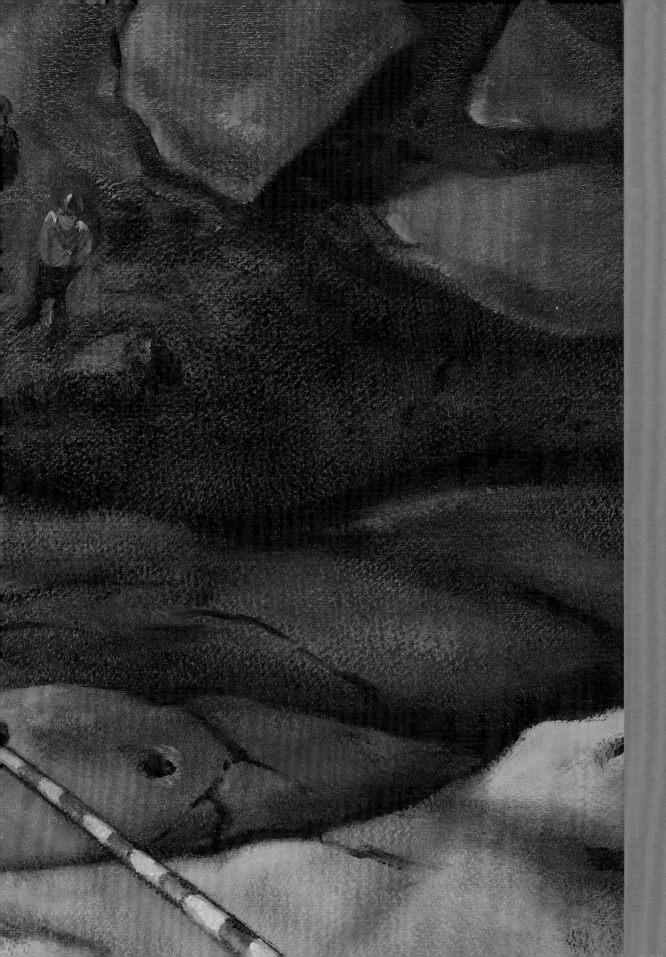

More and more climbers are pushing the limits of rock climbing by going higher, faster, and more extreme in every way. There are several different types of rock climbing. In the traditional form, as climbers mover higher they place and remove protective devices that are designed to stop a fall. In lead climbing, the climber takes the rope up with her—as opposed to top-rope climbing, where the rope is anchored above the climb. Sport climbing involves using pre-placed bolts for fast climbing. Free soloing is the dangerous act of climbing without any ropes at all. During multiday climbs up enormous walls, climbers even sleep in midair on portable hanging ledges.

Another popular activity, bouldering, involves carefully choosing handholds and footholds to scale giant boulders. In fact, climbing doesn't even have to involve going up (canyoneering is climbing down into canyons), and it doesn't require rocks. Climbing enthusiasts scale artificial walls, huge spruce or fir trees, and even the sides of buildings!

R r

S

Soaring with a sweeping view
while standing on a board.
S is the sport of Skysurfing.
Don't forget to pull the cord!

The sport of skydiving—jumping out of an airplane, freefalling, and then parachuting to safety—has been enjoyed by thousands of adventurous souls of all ages, from preschoolers to 101-year-olds. Far less common, but even more extreme, is the sport of skysurfing, a kind of skydiving in which divers attach a small board to their feet and perform aerial stunts during freefall. Advanced skysurfers can perform rolls, loops, and helicopter spins, but they are very difficult feats. Each skyboard has a releasable binding system so that the skysurfers can let go of the board if they lose control of it.

Competitive skysurfing is a team sport consisting of the skysurfer and a camera flyer, who wears a helmet with a video camera attached to it and records the stunts for the judges to examine. As world champion skysurfer Tony Hartman once said, "Without a camera flyer, there's nobody skysurfing. There's no way to prove you did it."

Swimming, cycling, running—
a grueling three-sport meet,
T is for Triathlon,
quite a sporting feat.

Imagine swimming more than two miles... or pedaling a bicycle for more than 100 miles... or running a marathon. Now imagine doing all three in a row! That's a triathlon, an event made up of three very challenging endurance sports. Thousands of triathlons are held around the world each year. The most famous is the Hawaii Ironman Triathlon, which was the first modern long-distance triathlon event in 1978 and now serves as the Ironman world championship. It requires competitors to swim 2.4 miles, bike 112 miles, and then run 26.2 miles.

There are various triathlon distances besides the Ironman, including the Half-Ironman, Olympic distance triathlons (about a one-fourth as long as the Ironman), and sprint triathlons (half as long as the Olympic event). There are also a series of off-road triathlons featuring swimming, mountain biking, and trail running. Although any triathlon is very competitive, many triathletes consider the event a success if they can complete the course. To finish is to win.

T t

Unbelievable! The ultimate!
The race goes on and on.
U is an endurance event
called an Ultramarathon.

Many people consider running a marathon to be the ultimate endurance feat. But for the nearly 15,000 people who compete in an ultramarathon each year, those 26.2 miles are only the beginning. Most ultramarathons are 50-mile or 100-mile (or kilometer) events, although some are even longer. Often they are courses on trails through the wilderness. For instance, the prestigious Western States 100 is a grueling 100-mile race in California's Sierra Nevadas involving about 40,000 feet of climbs and descents.

Perhaps the most famous of these events is the Badwater Ultramarathon, which has been called "the world's toughest footrace." It starts in the Badwater Basin in California's Death Valley, the lowest point in the Western Hemisphere at 282 feet below sea level. It ends 135 miles later at an elevation of 8,360 feet, more than halfway up Mount Whitney, the state's highest peak. The race usually takes place in July, when temperatures are most extreme—as high as 126 degrees! Generally, the top finisher completes the race in 24 to 28 hours!

V Vert skating and Vert riding
are V in our alphabet.
Show us a smooth varial.
How much air can you get?

Although **V** is for vert riding, the sport generally takes place on a ramp shaped like the letter U. Skateboarders and bicycle motocross (BMX) riders perform aerial tricks while riding back and forth along a half-pipe, a pair of curved ramps facing each other with a flat surface in between. These vert ramps are generally at least eight feet tall and curve steeply so that they are vertical near the top, allowing athletes to "catch air" and attempt challenging tricks. The flat ground in between ramps gives the rider time to regain his or her balance after landing.

One vert riding trick is a basic varial. In skateboarding, this is an aerial move where the board is spun from backward to forward beneath the feet. In BMX riding, a body varial is when the rider rotates 360 degrees off the bike, while the bike does a 180-degree turn in the air.

A wild, raging river,
a wet, wondrous show,
W in our alphabet
is a Whitewater rodeo.

Whitewater rodeo, also known as play-boating or freestyle kayaking, has been described as gymnastics on water. A competitor paddles his or her kayak into a "hole" in a fast-moving river where water drops quickly and then swirls rapidly, making it possible to stay there instead of floating downstream. While remaining in the hole as long as possible, the play-boater performs a series of tricks and maneuvers—including surfing, spinning, loops, and cartwheels—and receives a score from judges.

In whitewater racing, the object is to pilot a kayak down a river as fast as possible. Sometimes, this means simply running the rapids from point A to point B. Or it may mean negotiating a slalom course featuring 20 or 25 gates (poles suspended vertically over the river). River rapids are generally divided into six main classes according to the speed of the current, the steepness, and the number of hazards. These categories range from Class I (easy) to Class VI (highly dangerous).

The X Games are a multisport event, nationally televised on ESPN, celebrating the thrills and spills of extreme sports—under the summer sun and on winter snow. The Summer Games, held each year since 1995, take place in Los Angeles, California. The event features skateboarding, wakeboarding, surfing, motocross, and BMX freestyle competitions. The Winter Games, which began in 1997, draw more than 200 competitors to the area in and around Aspen, Colorado, where the lineup of sports includes skiing, snowboarding, and SnoCross (riders catching big air on snowmobiles!). A number of extreme sports were featured in past X Games, but are no longer part of the competition—everything from in-line skating and street luge to bungee jumping and skysurfing. Often the X Games provide a showcase for tricks never accomplished before. For instance, during the 1999 Summer X Games, legendary skateboarder Tony Hawk finally landed a 900-degree spin!

X is for the X Games.
Go for bronze, silver or gold
in the summer heat
or the winter cold.

Y y

Skim over the waves
with a sail unfurled.
Y is for a Yacht race
all around the world.

A leisurely afternoon aboard a sailboat isn't very extreme, but a 35,961-mile race around the world certainly is. That was the length of the 2005–2006 Volvo Ocean Race, a seven-month competition featuring seven boats, each 70 ½ feet long with 10 crew members. Boats scored points for each leg finish, for passing certain checkpoints first and for winning races in various ports. The sailors took turns in four-hour shifts as they steered the boat and constantly adjusted the sails to adapt to the wind. The course, which included nine legs separated by brief rest stops, took the sailors around Africa and South America, across three oceans, past glaciers, and through thunderstorms. At one point one boat took on water up to the sailors' shins. Another boat turned on its side in the middle of the night on the way to Brazil. And one sailor broke his tailbone when a large wave washed over the deck. Now that's extreme!

A zip line is a means of getting from one place to another by using gravity. It consists of a pulley suspended from an inclined cable. A person can go from the top to the bottom of the cable by holding onto the freely moving pulley. Zip lines come in various sizes. Some are short and low and can even be found on children's playgrounds. Others are very long and very high, requiring the rider to wear a safety harness. These kinds of zip lines can be found all over the world. Adventurers can move at nearly 50 miles per hour along a 1,100-foot-long zip line above a rushing creek in the ski resort of Whistler, British Columbia, or they can glide across a rocky canyon in California's Mojave Desert on a zip line 500 feet long and 90 feet high. One of the most spectacular zip lines crosses Batoka Gorge, which was formed by another Z—the Zambezi River, bordering the African countries of Zambia and Zimbabwe.

Between Zambia and Zimbabwe,
there's quite a sight to see.
Zoom along a Zip line.
That's our letter Z.

Z
z

Brad Herzog

Brad Herzog lives on California's Monterey Peninsula with his wife Amy and his two sons, Luke and Jesse. As a freelance writer, Brad has won several awards from the Council for the Advancement and Support of Education, including a Grand Gold Medal for best magazine article of the year. Among the extreme sports he has written about are rock climbing and mountaineering, sled dog racing and drag racing, triathlons and ultramarathons.

Brad also has published more than two dozen books, including two memoirs about his travels through small-town America and five other alphabet books for Sleeping Bear Press—about soccer (*K is for Kick*), baseball (*H is for Home Run*), football (*T is for Touchdown*), golf (*P is for Putt*), and stock car racing (*R is for Race*). More information about Brad's books and his school visit program can be found at www.bradherzog.com.

Melanie Rose

Illustrator Melanie Rose's charming and lively oil paintings have graced the pages of several Sleeping Bear Press titles including *H is for Home Run: A Baseball Alphabet*; *K is for Kick: A Soccer Alphabet*; *Z is for Zamboni: A Hockey Alphabet*; and *A is for Axel: An Ice Skating Alphabet*. Melanie is a graduate of the Ontario College of Art. She makes her home in Mississauga, Canada, with her son Liam and their two cats, Mickey and Meesha.